Cornhole

Jessica Coupé

Backyard Games

AV2

www.openlightbox.com

Step 1
Go to **www.openlightbox.com**

Step 2
Enter this unique code

YRXLGYC42

Step 3
Explore your interactive eBook!

AV2

AV2 is optimized for use on any device

Your interactive eBook comes with...

Contents
Browse a live contents page to easily navigate through resources

Audio
Listen to sections of the book read aloud

Videos
Watch informative video clips

Weblinks
Gain additional information for research

Slideshows
View images and captions

Try This!
Complete activities and hands-on experiments

Key Words
Study vocabulary, and complete a matching word activity

Quizzes
Test your knowledge

Share
Share titles within your Learning Management System (LMS) or Library Circulation System

Citation
Create bibliographical references following the Chicago Manual of Style

This title is part of our AV2 digital subscription

1-Year 3–8 Subscription
ISBN 978-1-7911-3306-1

Access hundreds of AV2 titles with our digital subscription.
Sign up for a FREE trial at **www.openlightbox.com/trial**

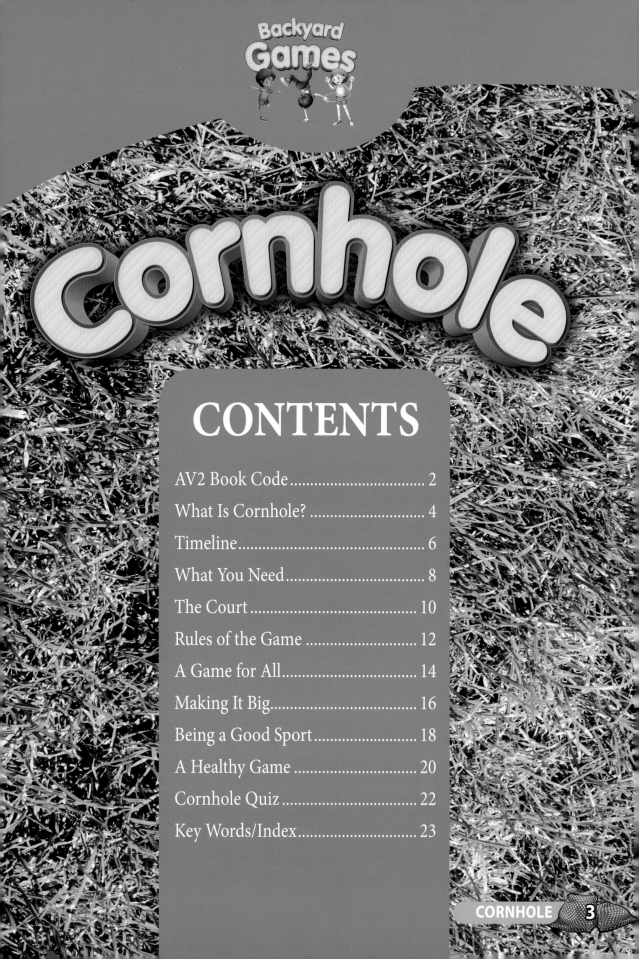

Backyard Games

Cornhole

CONTENTS

What Is Cornhole?

When the sun is shining and the weather is warm, people often head outdoors for a bit of fun. Sometimes, this fun is found in their own backyards. Playing games in the backyard gives families and friends a chance to relax and enjoy each other's company.

One popular backyard game is called cornhole. The goal of the game is to throw, or "pitch," a corn-filled bag into the hole of a slanted board. Points are scored if the bag lands on the board or falls through the hole.

The origin of cornhole is uncertain. According to legend, cornhole began as a children's game in Europe and was taken to the United States by **immigrants**. Other people think Native Americans invented the game. Still others think it evolved from an earlier game called **parlor quoits**.

Over the last 20 years, it has become very popular. In fact, cornhole is now a **professional sport**.

Cornhole is likely named after the dried corn used to fill the square bags that are thrown during the game.

Timeline

Cornhole has been a source of recreation and fun for a wide variety of groups over the years. From children to seniors, cornhole has kept many people entertained.

An early version of cornhole is played in Germany. German immigrants later bring this version to the United States.

1300s

1883

Heyliger de Windt **patents** a version of a game called parlor quoits. Played indoors, the game involves throwing beanbags into the hole of a slanted board.

1974

An article about a game similar to cornhole appears in the *Popular Mechanics* magazine. The concept of cornhole becomes better known. The game is initially played in the U.S. Midwest before expanding to other parts of the country.

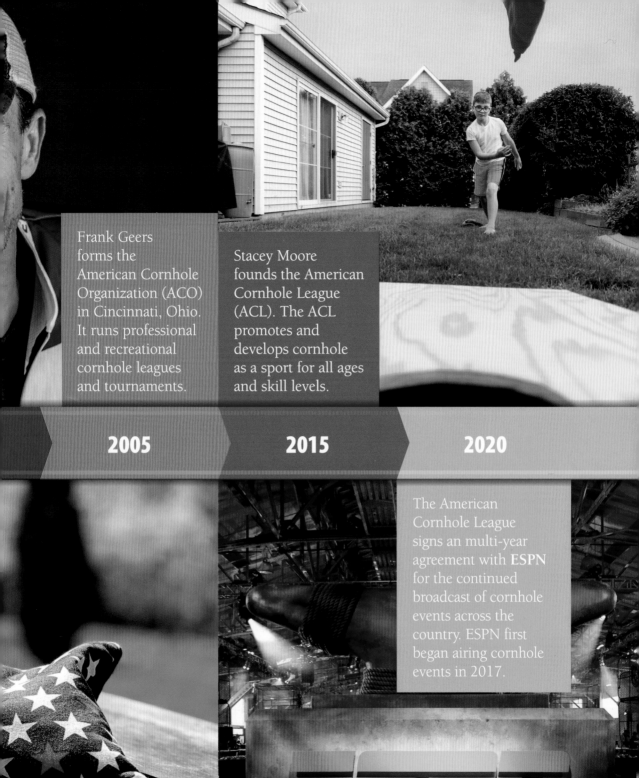

Frank Geers forms the American Cornhole Organization (ACO) in Cincinnati, Ohio. It runs professional and recreational cornhole leagues and tournaments.

Stacey Moore founds the American Cornhole League (ACL). The ACL promotes and develops cornhole as a sport for all ages and skill levels.

2005

2015

2020

The American Cornhole League signs an multi-year agreement with **ESPN** for the continued broadcast of cornhole events across the country. ESPN first began airing cornhole events in 2017.

What You Need

Cornhole requires only a few pieces of special **equipment**. The game can be fairly inexpensive to play. Players will need two cornhole boards and eight cornhole bags—four for each player. People may purchase cornhole sets in local shops or online. Industrious people can even make their own.

Optional cornhole equipment may include a score sheet and **carrying case**. Both of these can be made at home or bought online. Lights can also be added to cornhole boards.

A cornhole board has foldable legs. When set up, the board should slant toward the players.

Cornhole Board
Most cornhole boards are made of wood. They are about 48 inches (122 centimeters) in length and 24 inches (61 cm) wide with a 6-inch (1 cm) hole near the top.

Cornhole Bags
Cornhole bags are about 6 x 6 inches (15 x 15 cm) square, made of durable fabric, and filled with 16 ounces (450 grams) of dried corn. Professional bags are often filled with **resin pellets**.

Lights
Round lights are designed to fit into the hole in the board so players can still see the target even when the game is happening at night.

Score Sheet and Pencil
Remembering the points scored may be difficult for players. A score sheet and pencil helps players record and track points.

The Court

Cornhole games take place on a playing field called a **court**. When playing a game in the backyard, the court can be whatever size works best. To play an official ACO game, the court must be a level rectangular area between 8 and 10 feet (2.4 and 3 m) wide and 40 and 45 feet (12 and 13.75 m) long. Each court has three main features. These are the cornhole boards, the pitching boxes, and the **foul lines**.

The court has two lanes, each one containing a pitching box at either end of the court. The pitching box is where the players stand when they are ready to pitch the cornhole bags. Pitching boxes are about 4 feet by 3 feet (1.2 by 0.9 m) in area. Sandwiched in between the pitching boxes are the cornhole boards. They are known as the headboard and the footboard. The game starts at the headboard.

Players always pitch from the box on opposite side of the board to their opponents.

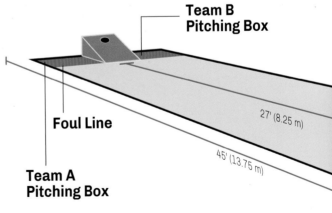

Team B Pitching Box

Foul Line

Team A Pitching Box

27' (8.25 m)

45' (13.75 m)

A cornhole court can be set up very easily. The foul lines and pitching boxes do not need to be marked on the ground.

The foul lines line up with the front edge of the cornhole boards. For adult players, the foul lines are 27 feet (8.25 m) apart. For players age 12 and under, the foul lines are only 12 to 15 feet (3.5 to 4.5 m) apart.

A court may be set up inside or outside. It can be on cement or lawn or sand. The only requirement is that it is on a level surface.

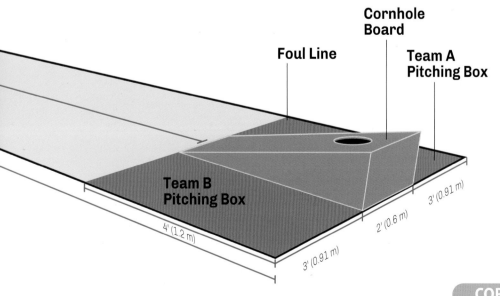

Cornhole Board

Foul Line

Team A Pitching Box

Team B Pitching Box

4' (1.2 m)

3' (0.91 m)

2' (0.6 m)

3' (0.91 m)

Rules of the Game

Two or four people can play cornhole. A game that has two people playing against each other is called singles. If four people are playing as teams of two, the game is called doubles.

Taking Turns

A coin toss decides who starts. From the headboard, players takes turns pitching a bag at the board on the opposite side of the court. They keep going until they have pitched all four bags. This is called an inning.

Getting Points

Players gain one point if the bag lands on top of the cornhole board. This is called "bag-in-the-court," or a "woody." Players get three points if their bag lands in the hole or is knocked into the hole by another bag. This is called "bag-in-the-hole," or "cornhole." A player at the footboard keeps score.

Foul

Players forfeit the inning if they get a foul. Fouls happen for many reasons. It is considered a foul if a player steps outside the pitching box as they throw. It is also a foul if the bag touches the ground, or an object, before landing on the board.

Score a Game

The winner of an inning is the player or team with the most points after all bags are pitched. The points achieved by the opponents are then subtracted from the winner's points to calculate the winner's score for that inning. A player or team wins the whole game by getting a total of 21 points.

For fairness, all players pitch from the same distance from the board. That distance can be adjusted to match the age and skill of the players.

A Game for All

Cornhole is very easy to learn how to play. This is one of the reasons it is becoming more and more popular. People of all backgrounds, ages, and skill levels can enjoy the game. This makes it an ideal game for families and friends to play in their backyards.

It is estimated that 25 million people, worldwide, play cornhole. Most of these people just play for fun. Besides backyards, cornhole is enjoyed in many other places where people gather. These include beaches, parks, sports centers, schools, and seniors' centers.

Many communities have cornhole clubs, where members can enjoy the game regularly. The clubs are made up of different divisions based on age and gender. For example, there are groups for men, women, and seniors.

Cornhole teams can be made up of players of any age.

No special clothing or footwear is needed to play cornhole.

Cornhole courts can easily be adjusted depending on who is playing. Children under 12 can play closer to the cornhole board than adults. Seniors and other groups have also adapted the official rules to suit their unique needs. The game's adaptability makes it easy for a range of people to enjoy playing cornhole.

Impressive!

In 2020, **Matt Pleil** scored **412 cornholes** in one hour.

Good Shot!

The **longest cornhole shot** ever made is **62 feet 6 inches** (19.05 m).

Making It Big

While cornhole is a popular leisure activity, it is also a competitive sport. The best players participate in official tournaments with the hope of becoming a cornhole champion. Competitions bring in players from across the country and around the world.

The ACO is the official governing body of cornhole. It hosts the World Championships of Cornhole each year. The ACL hosts its own World Championships. This competition receives special attention because it is broadcast on ESPN.

Cornhole tournaments are held across the country. The best players get the chance to become a professional.

Matt Guy

Matt Guy grew up in a competitive family. When he was in his teens, Matt began playing horseshoes with his father. Eventually, Matt switched to the game of cornhole.

Since then, Matt has won more than 1,000 cornhole tournaments. This includes being crowned ACO King of Cornhole nine times. Matt is known as the GOAT of Cornhole for his many wins. "GOAT" means "Greatest of All Time."

Matt has shared his passion for the game with his son, Bret. One of Matt's greatest moments was winning the ACO doubles with Bret as his partner. Bret Guy also won the ACO King of Cornhole title in 2013.

Being a Good Sport

Cornhole can be fun to play. It can also be dangerous if players are not careful. It is important that players follow the rules and be aware of what is happening around them. This will help keep people safe from injury.

Pitching should only be done in assigned areas. When not pitching, players should stand back from the court. They should also practice fair play by not distracting or disturbing other players. In professional tournaments, it is against the rules to make disturbing noises or movements. No one should move onto the court until the inning is done.

Even though cornhole is often an informal game between friends, it is important to play by the rules.

Playing fairly and not distracting opponents makes the game more fun for everyone.

Cornhole is a game that all ages can play. However, for some smaller players, the cornhole bags may be too heavy to throw. Some stores and organizations sell smaller, lighter cornhole bags for children. This allows a variety of people to enjoy the game.

Smaller children might need to stand nearer to the board to be able to hit it with their bags.

A Healthy Game

Cornhole is a pleasant way for people to get some exercise. It requires bending, reaching, and throwing. These movements are beneficial for the heart.

There are many potential health benefits to playing cornhole. Regular play helps players develop arm and leg muscles, strength, and flexibility. Often, cornhole is played outside so players get the benefit of fresh air, sunshine, and green space.

A game of cornhole can be enjoyed any time of the day and provide a bit of exercise.

Playing cornhole can also have a positive effect on mental health. It is a competitive, challenging sport, which stimulates the brain. Cornhole helps improve focus and attention. Players learn patience and planning skills. As players interact with others, they may also improve their mood and reduce their stress.

Cornhole helps people maintain a healthy body while having some fun at the same time.

Although cornhole is a simple game to learn, that does not mean it is easy to master. Professional players often practice throwing cornhole bags for hours at a time. With practice, players can develop their hand-eye coordination and improve their pitching skills.

Step-by-Step

It is about **16 steps** from one end of the standard **cornhole court** to the other.

Heavy!

Four cornhole bags weigh as much as a **4-pound** (1.8 kg) weight.

Cornhole Quiz

1 What is inside a cornhole bag?

2 How many people worldwide play cornhole?

3 How many cornhole bags does each player receive?

4 What is a cornhole playing field called?

5 How many times was Matt Guy crowned ACO King of Cornhole?

6 What does ACL stand for?

7 How can cornhole be adapted for children?

8 How many points are needed to win a game of cornhole?

Key Words

carrying case: a case or bag used to carry something from one place to another

court: the playing field of a cornhole game

equipment: the items needed to play a game

ESPN: the Entertainment and Sports Programming Network, which broadcasts sporting events

foul lines: lines that a player must not step over when throwing cornhole bags

immigrants: people who move from one country to another

parlor quoits: an indoor game involving throwing a beanbag at a hole in a board

patents: obtains the right to make, use, and sell an invention

professional sport: a sport in which participants are paid money

resin pellets: small pieces of hard plastic

Index

Get the best of both worlds.

AV2 bridges the gap between print and digital.

The expandable resources toolbar enables quick access to content including **videos**, **audio**, **activities**, **weblinks**, **slideshows**, **quizzes**, and **key words**.

Animated videos make static images come alive.

Resource icons on each page help readers to further **explore key concepts**.

Published by Lightbox Learning
276 5th Avenue, Suite 704 #917
New York, NY 10001
Website: www.openlightbox.com

Library of Congress Cataloging-in-Publication Data

Names: Coupé, Jessica, author.
Title: Cornhole / Jessica Coupé.
Description: New York, NY : AV2, 2022. | Series: Backyard games | Includes index. | Audience: Grades 2-3
Identifiers: LCCN 2021030396 (print) | LCCN 2021030397 (ebook) | ISBN 9781791142209 (library binding) | ISBN 9781791142216 (paperback) | ISBN 9781791142223
Subjects: LCSH: Cornhole (Game)--Juvenile literature.
Classification: LCC GV1097.C67 C68 2022 (print) | LCC GV1097.C67 (ebook) | DDC 790.1/5--dc23
LC record available at https://lccn.loc.gov/2021030396
LC ebook record available at https://lccn.loc.gov/2021030397

Printed in Guangzhou, China
1 2 3 4 5 6 7 8 9 0 25 24 23 22 21

082021
101120

Project Coordinator Heather Kissock
Designer Terry Paulhus

Photo Credits
Every reasonable effort has been made to trace ownership and to obtain permission to reprint copyright material. The publisher would be pleased to have any errors or omissions brought to its attention so that they may be corrected in subsequent printings. AV2 acknowledges Getty Images, Alamy, iStock, Shutterstock, Dreamstime, Matt Guy, and Frank Geers/American Cornhole Organization as its primary photo suppliers for this title.